The Big Book of Gratitude

Katherine P. Dacanay

Dedication

This book is dedicated to everyone walking through their own unraveling, to those counting pennies for gas money, learning bus routes with worn-out shoes, and wondering if the hard days will ever end.

To the ones sleeping in motel rooms who still make the bed each morning, to those who've lost everything they thought defined them, and to anyone who's ever whispered, "What am I paying for in this life that caused me to suffer this much?"

To those still living with the weight of invisible burdens, to the ones who smile in public while crying in private, and to anyone who's been told their intuition, their sensitivity, their knowing was "made up", you are not alone. Your struggles are real, your gifts matter, and your story is unfolding exactly as it should.

To myself, for all the yesterdays that led to today.

To the silent warriors rebuilding with different blueprints, to those learning that grace often arrives in work clothes, and to anyone discovering that their darkest chapters were preparing them for their most important work, this is for you.

To all my readers, who find their stories within the pages of this book.

May these pages remind you that rock bottom can become your foundation, that walking through fire can reveal your unshakeable core, and that the life waiting beyond your current struggles is truly extraordinary.

You are seen. You are guided. And you are never, ever alone.

Preface

There comes a moment in life when everything you thought was stable suddenly collapses, not to punish you, but to awaken you. For me, that moment arrived quietly, then all at once. What felt like a series of losses, disappointments, and heartbreaks became the very path that led me back to myself, back to God, and back to a life I didn't even know I was allowed to dream about.

This book was not planned. It was born from whispers, nudges, and divine redirection. It came from nights when I prayed for clarity, mornings when I begged for strength, and days when the only thing that kept me moving was a small voice inside saying, *"Trust Me. Keep going."* I did not write these chapters from a place of perfection or certainty — I wrote them from the middle of rebuilding, from a space of surrender, and from the quiet realization that God had been guiding me long before I ever understood His plan.

Every page reflects a piece of my journey: the breaking, the awakening, the learning, the unlearning, and the slow but sacred process of becoming whole. I share these moments not because I have all the answers, but because I finally learned how to listen. I learned that the Holy Spirit speaks in ways we often overlook — through intuition, through stillness, through unexpected encounters, through endings disguised as beginnings, and through lessons wrapped in pain.

This book is a testimony of what happens when you choose to believe that nothing in your life is random. That the detours, delays, heartbreaks, and closed doors are not punishments but "divine setups" — intentional moments designed to realign you with your purpose. It is a reminder that everything you walk through is shaping you, preparing you, strengthening you, and guiding you toward a life of deeper faith, greater gratitude, and true abundance.

If you are holding this book, I believe you were meant to. My hope is that as you read my story, you find pieces of your own. I hope you discover that healing is not linear, transformation is not comfortable, and rebirth is not soft — but it is all worth it. And more importantly, I hope you realize you are never alone. God is always working, always speaking, always restoring, even when it feels like everything is falling apart.

This book is not an instruction manual — it is an invitation. An invitation to reflect, to surrender, to trust the whispers, to honor your own journey, and to believe that you, too, are being guided toward something greater.

May these chapters remind you of one simple truth: Life becomes extraordinary the moment you trust that every step — even the painful ones — is leading you somewhere beautiful.

Acknowledgment

I wish to begin by acknowledging the Divine Architect of my life, my compass and my protector. The journey that led to these pages began in a valley of shadows, where the Divine's light met me, turning what felt like rock bottom into the foundation of a divine new dawn. For every redirection and answered prayer, my heartfelt thanks.

In moments when life's burdens were heavy and the path ahead was unclear, the presence of the Divine Source became my cynosure and guide. I am endlessly thankful for the distinctness and faithfulness of Your communication. Your divine wisdom dispelled my fears, resolved my uncertainties, and instilled my pain with divine purpose.

My deepest gratitude to those who shared my journey and held me up when I couldn't stand on my own. Thank you to all my loved ones for every prayer, word of encouragement, and moment of belief. Your unconditional support has been my foundation.

To every person who has ever experienced heartbreak, disappointment, or the feeling of losing themselves, this book is for you. I see you. I understand the weight you carry. I know how impossible it can feel to rebuild when your faith has been shaken, and your spirit feels exhausted. My hope is that these chapters remind you that restoration is real, healing is possible, and God is always closer than you think.

My sincere gratitude to the strangers whose brief crossings illuminated my hardest seasons. Your simple gestures of a kind word or gentle smile were divine comfort, a confirmation that I was never alone.

I salute the version of myself who would not yield—the woman who navigated the depths of pain through tears and prayers, surrendering to the process and rising stronger. Thank you for listening to the whispers of your spirit and allowing God's story to be written through you.

This is a testimony of where faith meets surrender, where the deepest wounds become the doorway to healing, and where God steps in to help you reclaim your intended self.

Contents

Chapter 1:
Hey! Do You Have a Minute?

How are you?

Are you facing a season where everything seems to be going wrong, despite your best intentions and unwavering effort? Do you feel like you're constantly pushing against an invisible current, unable to grasp the success you're working so hard for? If so, you're in the right place.

The initial work on this book began roughly four years ago. However, the intervening years brought significant life events that diverted attention and made sustained focus difficult. The journey through hardship began over two decades ago, and it's taken time to understand its full meaning. By processing and understanding a personal journey of change, one becomes equipped to truly assist others.

The depth of personal evolution became the cornerstone for empowering others. The tapestry of a personal journey reveals itself with greater definition with every client. An insistent inner voice steered the moment: researching thoroughly, seeking out the perfect partners to pen this book, and finally unveiling the lessons learned.

This message is inspired by clients I have encountered, who are doing their best to navigate life but find themselves feeling stuck. They often come to sessions carrying a silent burden, longing for connection and reassurance that their experiences are not unique.

I want you to know something: you are never alone.

When a client walks into my office, I really never know what to expect. I trust in the spirit messages that come through automatic writing. When a message from spirit comes through that clients can validate and connect with, I see their facial expressions and the colors around them change. Often, the messages are uplifting, bringing reassurance that they do not have to carry the whole world on their own.

Having personally navigated similar journeys to some clients, the intensity of difficult periods is absolutely understood. This shared experience, alongside witnessing the remarkable resilience of women who've faced immense adversity, is inspiring. The people I meet are sweet and unassuming, needing just a little push and someone to share their thoughts with.

The approach in these sessions has evolved, allowing for deeper connections. Insightful and compassionate support is offered, fostering understanding through honest communication that is both gentle and impactful.

The increasing demand for intuitive services has led to a rewarding and busy practice, with clients reaching out from local, national, and international locations. Mastery of managing the schedule and energy has enabled personalized support across time zones.

Private client sessions are a truly rewarding experience, designed to ignite. Private client sessions are a deeply rewarding experience. They are designed to initiate profound healing while offering clarity and direction. Rather than providing answers, clients are guided to discover their own capabilities and resilience in the face of adversity.

My work involves connecting with a remarkable array of individuals, each possessing a different background, a distinct story, and unique concerns, spanning from young girls to women in their late eighties. It's a privilege to tune into their individual needs and to truly listen, learning from their diverse perspectives and guiding them effectively.

This season of life is nothing short of breathtaking. The remembrance of past pain only serves to heighten gratitude for the continuous love, support, and positive experiences that make the present so deeply treasured. Grateful to have endured challenges and emerged capable, the conscious efforts made were directed toward improving personal situations. In addition to working as an intuitive life coach, the ability to support clients with their real estate needs is possible, having obtained the license in 2019, prior to the pandemic.

Life has reached a state of profound calm – the ability to finally breathe deeply, to find restful sleep at night. This wasn't always the case, and the essential message for anyone facing their own struggles is this: persevere. What waits beyond the current challenges is truly worth the journey.

Navigating life can sometimes feel like driving a desolate road at night, with only your headlights illuminating the narrow path ahead. In those moments, when fear threatens to overwhelm, it's about channeling that fear into forward momentum, trusting that the light you carry within will guide you to where you need to be.

The hardships someone faces can become a powerful stepping stone, leading to the discovery of a confidence that lay dormant. Reflecting on a period of four years without a car, relying on public transit, learning the ins and outs of bus and VTA routes, and even experiencing temporary homelessness in a motel reveals how these challenging times honed adaptability and unearthed a deep reservoir of self-belief. What began as circumstances outside one's control surprisingly transformed into the very foundation for the positive events that followed.

In the midst of your most difficult times, when everything feels like it's falling apart, know that these can be the very moments that open doors to unforeseen grace and a powerful purpose. While it's tough to believe when you're in the thick of it, this is possible.

Forget the forced smiles and the platitude that everything happens for a reason. Some chapters of life are inherently complicated, painful, and unjust. However, the profound lesson learned is that within those shadows, tiny beacons ignite: gestures of kindness from unforeseen places, the revelation of inner strength someone didn't realize they possessed, and the wisdom of mentors who emerge from the most unlikely circumstances.

This journey was a tumultuous, persistent, and often brutal stripping away of all that was thought to define a person. It involved an ego-shattering process and the invaluable realization that accepting help was a profound act of self-preservation. The narrative is of discovering that the life painstakingly built lacked true stability, leading to the revelation of a far more substantial reality.

Yet, it's also about discovering that genuine confidence emanates from the reassurance found in the tapestry of our lives, and in an unceasing gratitude to God for the entirety of our journey – both the seasons of plenty and the leaner times – embracing this thankfulness as a fundamental way of being, a constant dialogue with the divine.

If someone feels like the world is conspiring against them or they're trapped in the worst possible circumstances, these feelings are temporary. The frustration of giving your all yet still feeling stuck is understood.

Moving from my old place to the new one taught me a valuable lesson about people's hidden strength. It made me realize that help can come in different forms, from what we expect and from the people we have not looked at. It revealed that the potential for change is much greater than the tough situation we are in.

So, in fact, what I mean by "Hey! Do you have a minute?" is: are you ready to hear a story about how one of the worst periods in someone's life became the gateway to the most important one? Are you willing to consider the fact that your present difficulties may be the steps for the wonderful things that are yet to come?

Sharing a story is an act of vulnerability, as some chapters can be deeply challenging to navigate and recount. It is offered in the belief that any journey, whatever its current struggles, holds profound importance. Know that in moments of feeling lost, overwhelmed, or unfairly burdened, one is truly never alone.

Even when your headlights seem like the only light in the darkness, remember to trust in the inner guidance that is being brought to you at the moment. Continue moving forward, and allow someone to share the experience from that challenging road. Because where someone is headed is far more extraordinary than anything that can be glimpsed from the current vantage point.

I think it's time to seize this moment…

Chapter 2:
The Life I Built
(And Thought Was Solid)

My life seemed absolutely reasonable for more than twenty-five years. I supported medical directors while working in corporate healthcare, waking up early to avoid the traffic and settling into the familiar 8-to-5 routines. Those 40-to-60-hour weeks established my routine, and overtime was a frequent companion when the task demanded. I worked in similar roles at several large hospitals, establishing what I thought was a steady career.

There was something deeply satisfying about those days. I had put in hard work, and at the end of those days, I felt good about supporting the Medical Directors. I held the same positions in different medical organizations, building consistency in my career one hospital at a time.

Home has always been a calm and welcoming place to return to after a long day when I think about that time, home represented sanctuary – that precious moment of walking through the door and finally being able to exhale.

But let me be honest about something: stability was still being built. The financial struggles were real, and it was often difficult to make ends meet. But I coped and made it work. Difficult times for me are when you have to count pennies and hope you have enough for gas money. Those were the moments that tested everything I thought I was building.

Security, for me, was more financial. I believed that money can really improve lives and, in turn, elevate emotions to a more positive way of thinking. It seemed so clear then – if I could solidify the financial foundation, everything else would fall into place.

I was working toward a master's degree, hoping to elevate myself in the corporate world. I found the plan to be very sensible and attainable. Gaining more education would open up better opportunities, bringing the stability I sought by putting in so much effort. My short-term plans were simple: I had made a couple of trips, but they were only to visit my family, who lived two hours away.

Despite working toward these goals, I still felt that something was missing. It seemed restricted. I was convinced there was a lot more to life than what I was going through at the time. So, I kept on trekking and working really hard. I also took on part-time retail and restaurant positions to make ends meet, determined to push through whatever held me back.

In retrospect, I can see the warning indicators attempting to draw my attention. Although I have worked full-time in the past, I have had a few layoffs and job losses over my career in the medical sector.

When it became challenging to cope with the emotional and financial hardships, and I had no one to turn to, I knew that something had to change. I saw the same cycle repeat itself – I would get a job, then the company would downsize, and I would lose my job. Then, I would start over again, leaving me no room to improve my finances.

The worst was when I was diagnosed with cancer. I took time off to heal, I was laid off, then I lost my cars through repossession, and I lost a place to live. It was as if everything I'd worked so hard to build was being stripped away, piece by piece.

My natural optimism made it difficult for me to accept what was happening. It took a while for me to reach a point in my life where I could accept that things can change instantly.

I have very few friends, and it was difficult for me to confide in them about what I was going through. I took it all in and stayed silent. I kept my problems intact and had to work through them calmly.

However, something interesting began to emerge during this time. I found myself with the space to reflect, and during that period, I learned to meditate and explore deeper states of awareness. I learned about energy healing, and honestly, I'm still not sure how I ended up meeting my Reiki teacher. Looking back, I realized I was being guided.

There's a beautiful irony in how life unfolds. I had initially planned to retire in corporate healthcare, but apparently, there were other plans for my life.

Soon, as I followed guidance, I was led to learn other forms of healing. I was gifted tuition to attend the Kerala Ayurveda Academy by a doctor I used to work with, who now considers me part of their family, and I've claimed them as mine. I graduated with an Ayurveda Health Counselor degree.

The moment when I first sensed my "solid life" beginning to shake was during those times when I would get a job and then lose it through company downsizing. There was no stability. The emotions that stood out most clearly were disappointment, confusion, and fear. Those were difficult years, and staying calm and trusting that things would turn for the better soon became my daily practice. Prayer and gratitude were what held me together.

I didn't realize then that this complete dismantling of everything I thought was solid was preparing me for something I couldn't have imagined. The life I had built, which I thought was so reasonable and achievable, was just the foundation for something far more extraordinary.

At times, we perceive our things as being destroyed, putting them in the proper order. However, I was not able to realize this at that moment. I saw all my efforts losing their hold on me, leaving me to think about what would be left after the dust had settled.

The universe, it seemed, had very different plans for my master's degree than I did. And those plans would require me to learn lessons that no classroom could teach – lessons that could only be learned by walking through the fire of losing everything and discovering what remains when all the external securities are stripped away.

Looking back, I can now see that the life I built wasn't as solid as I thought. But I didn't know then that this was exactly the point. Some foundations need to crumble so that something unshakeable can be built in their place.

The woman who counted pennies for gas money, who worked multiple jobs just to make ends meet, who faced cancer and job loss and homelessness, was being prepared for a calling she couldn't yet imagine. The experiences that felt like failures were the curriculum for a life of service that would touch hearts across time zones.

But I'm getting ahead of myself. First, there was the unraveling to navigate, and the lessons that could only be learned in the space between losing everything and discovering what truly cannot be taken away.

Chapter 3:
When Everything Started Unraveling

Sometimes, life is an extreme division of all you know into "before" and "after." A call from the doctor that I had when driving home from work was just one of those moments.

While heading home, I was worried the whole time thinking about my test results. I was anxiously waiting for a call from the doctor's office. When my phone finally rang, and I saw their number, I didn't hesitate. I answered immediately, even though I was still driving. What the doctor told me in that moment would change my life.

They said, "We got your test back, and it is positive. You have cancer."

Pure shock! I could not say anything. I had so many questions in my mind. What now? How long do I have? I will never forget how wrong it felt for a doctor to deliver such life-altering news over the phone. There was no care, no compassion. I was just driving, and with a few words, my entire life changed.

The change to my everyday life and work hit me hard. I felt shocked at first. That feeling turned into worry. I knew I had to think about what to do next. When I saw the specialist, they recommended that I undergo chemotherapy. But deep down, I thought chemo was not right for me at all. I said no. The specialist kept telling me it could help, but I kept saying no. Then, after I refused again and again, she told me about a test that could show what treatment would be good for me.

The test results confirmed that I was right to trust my instinct.

So I found myself facing six weeks of full radiation treatments, daily sessions for an hour each day at 6 a.m. The emotions and thoughts that stand out most clearly from that time centered around one desperate hope: this treatment has to work; it has to.

And it did.

After my treatments, I had follow-up appointments where I was told I had to be on a "chemo" pill for the rest of my life. Once again, I refused.

I promised myself that I would never miss any doctor's appointments, and to complement these visits, I also used energy medicine, acupuncture, chiropractic medicine, and Ayurveda. At the end, the diagnosis that I had been asking for appeared: I was given the green light from cancer. I don't have cancer anymore!

Yet, the cancer diagnosis was only the beginning of the chain reaction.

The series of events that followed is still very vague for me as I am trying to recall them, and it also seems that they happened a long time ago, but I am sure that everything had changed in less than a year. I was still working at the ambulatory care when I received my diagnosis, but then I lost my job because the employer said I took too much time off. Looking back, I can see that the employer somewhat downplayed my situation, but I also realize that I fell into the victim mindset – *poor me, what now* – instead of fighting for my right to take the time off to care for myself.

Without my job, I was not able to pay for a place to live. I also lost my car because I could not make payments. Every loss made me feel less like myself. It shook my idea of who I am and what makes me feel safe. Being diagnosed with a health issue was the biggest shock for me at the beginning.

I was not worried about work then, as I thought I would find another job very soon. But the loss of more things made a bad situation worse. I was very exhausted and down in spirits. I felt like I didn't fit in anywhere. Even though I was in trouble, I was grateful to have people I could rely on and who supported me when I shared my experience.

Each loss made me look into the mirror to discover who I really am and how I recognize myself. It was a tough period, and I was very exhausted and low in spirits as I tried to recover. I had no idea how I could bounce back after everything went wrong with me. I asked God to give me the power to continue. I remained thankful for my life and for the things I still had. I believe I had to be strong if I ever thought about those days. I had to believe that better times were coming, and I continued to hold onto that hope as time went on.

The practical challenges of suddenly having nowhere to go were immediate and jarring. After I lost my job, I was receiving minimal assistance from disability insurance following my surgery. I visited my doctor, who assisted me in completing disability forms, and shortly after, I received financial support. But it wasn't enough for me to afford anything better than a shanty motel.

I was happy to have a place to stay out of the rain and to be safe. I had enough money to get something to eat and pay for the motel, but not having a car meant I had to travel around the town in a new way. I was supposed to figure out the city bus system, but because of my mistakes and taking the wrong bus lines, my trip back to the motel was delayed.

Maintaining my dignity and sense of self was very tough when everything familiar had disappeared. It was a drastic adjustment, learning to accept this new situation. Yet even in those difficult and humbling moments, something sustained me. I always felt that the Divine was looking after me. I always felt that I was being directed and paid attention to that guidance. I trusted, and as time went on, life started to feel better. Eventually, I got another job and was able to get an apartment.

Looking back now, I can see how one crisis seemed to create conditions for the next. When one recognizes the challenges they're facing and decides to rise above instead of going down the old path, that's when transformation becomes possible. It starts with our thoughts and how we value ourselves. When we reach a level of uncertainty where we have felt and lived at our lowest, believing that no matter what we do, nothing in our life will change, then nothing will ever change.

At the time, though, I was oblivious to this pattern. I didn't realize the spiritual aspects of why I was experiencing such traumatic events that felt like punishment. What was I supposed to learn? What was it like to have everything pulled from under my feet? I felt beaten down and hopeless.

How did I cope day by day? I walked a lot during those times in my worn-out running shoes. As time went by, every step I took encouraged me to keep going. I was grateful to have gained strength, and walking was good for me. Learning the bus routes taught me to be alert and keen to what was happening around me.

I learned to be safer and more vigilant about my surroundings.

Through this life experience, I developed an internal compass, allowing me to perceive my physical orientation and the ambient energies in all directions. My overall awareness expanded, and my breathing became more intentional and refined.

Sometimes I didn't know if the hard days would ever end. I would ask myself, "What's next?" and "When will this end?" However, over time, I started to think in ways that made me stronger. I discovered the worth of what I could do. I started writing a diary, and having my feelings out on paper was very good. This was my support during the hard times.

I didn't know then that things were going from bad to worse, even though it hurt me a lot. It was a process of my preparation for something I couldn't even imagine. Each and every loss and hard moment that would make me push myself more than I thought I could was teaching me lessons that no school could teach.

The woman who answered the phone while driving home from work was about to discover the secret strengths she had never known about.

Chapter 4:
Walking Through Town
(And Through My Pride)

The day I opened my savings account and saw the number that confirmed my worst fear is a day I can still feel in my bones. The disability benefits arrived like a small life raft. I was lucky to receive them, but they were not an anchor.

They were temporary breathing rooms, and I feared the bigger question: When, if ever, would I get a job again?

I knew I could work; I just had to learn to navigate life differently. I learned quickly that managing money down to the last coin became a job. I budgeted for basics and made searching for work into a full-time task. That rationed, anxious existence is the hard truth that ushered me into homelessness.

The losses came in sequence, cars gone, the townhouse gone, and suddenly there was no time to grieve how I thought I should. Practicality took over. I rented a moving truck, loaded what I could, and rented a storage unit near the motel where I'd soon live. I moved into that motel with two cats in tow.

I carried the necessary things for the cats and me, including a portable stove. Motel rules forbade cooking, but when the management left, and the hallway lights dimmed, I would warm a small meal and eat quietly. Survival required bending rules sometimes; dignity required keeping as much of my routine intact as possible.

I am still astonished at how methodical I became in those weeks. There was little time to feel bad, so I told myself that feeling could come later. There was laundry to do, bus passes to buy, and a constant tally in my head of coins, routes, and schedules. I was hypervigilant, always aware of my surroundings.

Was it paranoia?

Maybe.

Or maybe it was the natural caution of someone who has lost their base and needs to protect what little remains. The laundromat felt like a vulnerability ritual; sharing washers and dryers with strangers made me nervous in a way I'd never been before. I learned fast to watch the clocks and to know when to signal the bus driver that my stop was next. Small things became lifelines.

Carrying my life in boxes and a few bags taught me a humility I hadn't planned to learn. The professional credentials, the polished resume, the years of steady work, all stayed with me in memory, but they didn't put food on the table or buy bus tokens.

People who saw me in simple clothing, in an early morning bus queue, or moving a tote into the motel did not know the medical credentials behind my name. I kept all of that to myself.

No one at work knew. I had never confided in people, not even close friends; only one trusted friend knew, and they kept my secret safe. So the stares I feared rarely happened outwardly, my concealment protected me from public assumptions, but the weight of imagined judgment was real enough. I carried what I needed physically, and the rest inside my head.

Family outreach was one of the largest tests of my pride. I tried to reach out to those closest to me, to say, "This is happening."

But our relationships were already strained. Before the diagnosis and the unraveling, my family and I were not on good terms; they disagreed with my life choices. I left messages, even one about my cancer diagnosis, and received no return calls. The silence felt like punishment.

I had been declared cancer-free after my surgery, a moment that should have brought relief and some shared joy, but instead it deepened the loneliness, as there was no family support even then. Shortly after, I refused the lifelong chemo pills, choosing instead to trust my own path forward.

I allowed myself to imagine dark possibilities: that I was being expelled, disowned, that if I had died, they would have thought I was a burden.

Those thoughts were corrosive. Yet I refused to be defeated by them. I told myself, again and again, that I was alive and grateful. I learned painfully to accept that I was on my own and fully trust the Divine's promise that I would be okay.

Emotionally, that lack of family support cut deep. I felt disowned and punished in ways I could not logically explain. But the practical steps I had taken, the rented storage, the motel, the methodical money management, meant I had to keep moving.

When I finally did find work again, I pushed even harder: when a job opportunity arose, I took a second job and worked three nights a week. Work became the scaffolding to rebuild a life. Through that relentless focus on day-to-day survival, the worst of the pain began to dull, bit by bit.

Daily survival during those months read like a list of small wars: keeping appointments, ensuring bills for the motel and food were paid, protecting my cats, learning bus timetables, and not missing a single chance to apply for open positions. No one at the offices where I worked knew my private life.

I walked the same halls, answered the same emails, and then returned to a motel room that smelled faintly of bleach and carpet. I kept my dignity by keeping my routine. I wrote in a diary, words on paper that acted like a friend, which helped me keep my head above the water. Writing was my secret ritual of sanity.

Amid the grinding routine and the daily vigilance, kindness glowed like small, impossible lanterns. I was led, through a sequence I could never fully map, to people who became anchors. I was guided to teachers in energy medicine and into courses that fed my soul. One application I sent, almost without expectation, changed everything.

A medical director needed an assistant. I applied for the position and was hired on the spot. That simple, immediate hiring is one of those rare fortune-turned-miracle moments that make you swallow hard and say, "Thank you."

The doctor's family treated me like one of their own. Blood isn't always family; sometimes family finds you. They eventually gifted me a year's schooling to attend the Kerala Ayurveda Academy, a scholarship that felt like grace. The courses were in English and Hindi, and the challenge of learning them opened a new corridor of possibilities. I graduated as an Ayurveda Health Counselor, and with each certification and each teacher I met, my intuitive abilities strengthened.

What surprised me most was how a crisis reveals people's true characters. Some of whom I expected to help were absent; some strangers offered compassion in the most ordinary acts. I cannot remember cruelty from expected sources in concrete detail; perhaps my memory protects me from cataloging every wound.

Instead, I remember the spiritual teachers, the strangers whose small mercies kept me moving, and the medical family who became my own. These contrasts taught me something essential: most people carry burdens in silence. This realization strengthened my resolve to be kind, listen attentively, and refrain from judgment. We rarely know the full story of the person standing beside us at the bus stop.

Rock bottom was not a single sharp point so much as a flattening across many areas of life, a season when everything happened at once. I remember the dizzying sense of defeat when all the external securities were stripped away: cars repossessed, a home gone, a job lost, the humiliation of sleeping somewhere not meant for long-term living. Words did not come easily then.

But beneath the ache, a single practical question began to rise: What do I do with what's left of me?

The answer was stubbornly simple: keep moving on.

It was not poetic. It was not heroic in the traditional sense. It was steady, small steps: walk to the bus stop, apply for jobs, show up at interviews, answer emails, keep the cats fed, make the bed if I could, and keep a diary. Walking became literal and symbolic. I often walked in my old running shoes, which taught me patience and endurance. Every step forward became an affirmation: I will try again tomorrow.

When I finally had enough to secure a place of my own and buy a used car, a car I still keep as a reminder, I allowed myself to feel what had been postponed for so long. I grieved. I sorted through the storage unit, rescued only the items that mattered, and donated the rest. Those actions felt like a ritual clearing: out with the excess, in with what remained true. That humble secondhand car became a talisman of resilience, a daily reminder that the worst chapter had been survived.

Walking through town during those months taught me more about myself and about people than many years of comfort ever could have. It humbled me, stripped away my pride, and taught me how to ask for nothing and accept help when it appeared.

Crisis revealed both the best and the worst in others, but more importantly, it revealed the quiet, unbreakable core inside me. When everything else fell away, the essential question, *'What will I do with what's left of me?'* found its answer in each small, stubborn step onward.

Chapter 5:
The Story I Told Myself About Why This Was Happening

Throughout those years, I was caught in the loop of my own heavy and haunting memories. I felt like I had to relive those terrible events all the time, as if by going through them again and again, maybe I could somehow alter the outcome. The heaviness that came with it was draining. I cried frequently - sometimes when I didn't expect it, sometimes during the long, lonely hours - but still, I had to go on with my life.

The thoughts that I had were not always about finding someone to blame. More often than not, they were focused on me, my questions, and my lack of answers.

The same question, again and again, was: What am I paying for in this life that caused me to suffer this much?

That question was like the refrain in a song, the main theme of my life that I was somehow responsible for, that through my suffering, some sort of invisible debt was being collected.

Out there among people, I was a different person. I knew how to present the best version of myself and show a calm face to the world. I didn't give my private pain the privilege of showing itself with full intensity to those outside. Nevertheless, I still thought that afflictions don't last forever and clung to that detestable little truth inside.

I was also very aware that I needed to change the narrative I was telling myself. Working with Dr. Andersen in our meditation sessions was one of those quiet but significant shifts. Slowly, life became more bearable with those practices, not all at once, not in big strides, but in small, noticeable changes. I still felt the load, but it was no longer as heavy as it used to be.

However, the mental cycle that kept coming back to my mind was equally exhausting. Certain moments triggered it sharply. When I finally managed to purchase a car and began driving again, something as ordinary as passing people on the street or seeing others at bus stops could pull me right back into the years when walking and public transit were my only options.

For four years, I had walked around town, planned routes according to bus timetables, and carried the exhaustion of that survival. Driving again should have been pure relief, but instead, it carried an echo of those struggles.

At the same time, gratitude did break through. When I started receiving a paycheck again, I remember the feeling of confidence returning, piece by piece. Financial stability, initially fragile, began to take shape, and that mattered deeply. The reminders of those four hard years did not drain me of strength; if anything, they gave me more.

They stood as proof that I had endured, and while life did not feel steady immediately, I can say with certainty that by about seven years after, I finally felt a lasting stability returning.

I never compared my situation to anyone else's. That thought never made sense to me. I always believed comparison was unfair, to myself and to others. Each person walks their own path. They have their challenges; I have mine. Life moves differently for all of us, and weighing my struggles against someone else's victories or losses would not have been helpful. That belief protected me in its own way.

Still, the victim mindset carried its own prison bars. I can see now how negativity clouded my mind during that time. When the loop of dark thoughts started, I didn't always know how to stop it or redirect it. That's when I began experimenting with self-talk. It may sound simple, but speaking out loud to myself gave me a way to listen differently.

When I heard my own words, I could pause and reflect:

Was that thought helping me?

Was it true?

Did I want to keep repeating it?

From there, I learned to reframe sentences and to turn harsh self-judgments into softer, more loving reminders.

Kindness from others did reach me during that period, though it was hard to accept. I often felt I had nothing to give in return. All I could offer was my time, a simple thank you, or my presence. Their thoughtful words and caring actions mattered deeply, but my own mindset sometimes blocked me from fully receiving them.

Looking back, I remember the helplessness, the moments when defeat seemed permanent. But I also remember the shift once I allowed myself to rebuild confidence. Of all things, laughter became part of my medicine. I watched countless funny movies just to lift my spirits.

That laughter wasn't superficial; it reminded me of who I had been before the heaviness set in. As I laughed more, I noticed something remarkable: happier people began to appear in my life. The light in me attracted light in others. Those friendships have lasted. Many people I met during that period are still in my life today. Some of these friends and I have formed deeper connections, and they are now my closest friends - friends I consider family.

I was in a situation where I had to unearth new perspectives on life and stop seeing myself as a victim. If I wanted to live, I had to change my viewpoint. No, it was not a change caused by a noticeable one-time event; it was a succession of small but profound moments that influenced change.

When the same stories creep up in my mind, I have learned to pause, breathe, and recognize that these are just thoughts. Thoughts that do not define me. I had to let go of the misfortunes I once believed caused these events, and I had to have faith that I could create something new from this moment onward.

Was I afraid?

Of course, yes.

I was scared of the changes that might be coming, both the positive and the negative ones. But courage is not the lack of fear; it is the decision to step forward despite the presence of fear. I gave myself the verdict that I must be courageous and put my full weight on that decision.

My perspective on life changed significantly after I started to take courses in self-help, spiritual growth, and various healing modalities. The learning process did indeed equip me with new resources, a new way of speaking, and ways to get to know and understand myself. I developed a much better understanding of my inner thoughts and feelings.

Love and gratitude were becoming more dominant than fear and doubt. If you asked me for the first words of encouragement I told myself during that time, I honestly could not tell you. Words fell short of what I felt. I remember the intensity of the feelings more: an eruption of love, an immersion of gratitude, and a stunning impression that life could be different.

This was the moment that allowed a real change of direction. I was no longer bound to the old narrative of suffering and punishment. I was on my way to living a new story I was learning, not the one that excluded pain, but rather one that included the same, along with strength, resilience, and the bravest decision to start over.

Chapter 6:
When Grace Shows Up
in Work Clothes

Staying at the motel was a weird mix of scary and comforting. The first days were really difficult. The cats were my major concern the whole time. How could they be comfortable in such a strange and different place, so far away from the familiar flow of our old house?

The room was basically the opposite of what you could call a comfortable place to stay. The air-conditioning unit always disturbed the quiet with its loud and rattling "protest" to the heat.

Every day, the cleaning staff would come and go with their carts, making noise, towels stacked high. Their existence indicated to me that this room was not mine and that we would not live in it for much longer. People checked out, the room was cleaned, and the next batch of strangers was here. It made me aware that this was not permanent and that things would change.

I had to become inventive, almost out of necessity. That little gas-powered stove I carried with me stopped being just a tool. It became my anchor. When you don't have a refrigerator, you can't live as most people do. The bed, for instance, wasn't much. A flat slab with fabric stretched over it. The pillows were more symbolic than functional.

Yet, I discovered that discomfort can be slightly bent, shaped by your hands. It isn't luxury, but it's enough. And once you realize that, even a hard surface yields to a bit of ingenuity, you stop waiting for perfect conditions and start creating tolerable ones.

Then there was cleaning. I didn't expect it to matter. But it became something almost ceremonial. Wiping a surface wasn't just wiping; it was staking a claim against the disorder pressing in from every side. It was as if every gesture, however small, said: here, in this square of space, I decide how things stand. That mattered. More than I would have admitted at the time, it steadied me.

Sometimes dark questions slipped in: *Is this all that life has to offer? Is this where I stay?*

That's when the spiral would threaten. But I forced myself to counter it. No, this is not permanent. This is a stage. You can endure this because there is something better ahead. Gratitude became the weapon I fought with. It wasn't grand gratitude; there were no sweeping victories to celebrate.

It was smaller, quieter: the warmth of my cats curling up beside me, a hot meal on that little stove, the plain fact that I was managing, each counted as evidence that despair didn't have the final say.

I was searching, not aimlessly, but deliberately, for someone I could talk to about the depression that clung to me. I leafed through names and numbers, setting appointments, and found most reached too quickly for the prescription pad. Now, I wasn't against medication, but I knew that wasn't the real answer for me.

Somewhere deep inside, I understood that what I needed wasn't just a chemical adjustment. I needed someone who could *see me* and speak to the deeper parts of my life, not just my symptoms.

Then I came across Dr. Andersen's name. When I called her office, she answered the phone herself. That, in itself, surprised me. She spoke with me for a while, not rushing, not dismissing. By the end of the call, she offered me an appointment for the following Thursday at 11 a.m.

I didn't know then how much that Thursday morning would alter the course of my journey.

Walking into her office for the first time, I immediately noticed her presence. Dr. Andersen was stern-looking, an older woman, she didn't smile much, and everything about her posture and tone suggested strength and firmness.

Our first meeting was only thirty minutes, a kind of orientation session. She began by listening to me intently, and she sensed that her usual formality and business approach would not be successful. As she listened to me, she customized my weekly session structure. Her voice was soft yet commanding, both comforting and firm. She was blunt and wasn't keen on listening to my long personal story.

She preferred brevity, clarity, and directness. In that first session, I didn't share my entire story, just fragments, just enough for her to begin forming her impressions.

Still, I remember the moment I walked through her office door. Something in me whispered, '*This is it, Katherine. This is a safe place. You can open up here.*'

At the end of that brief session, she said something that lodged itself deep inside me: *"Then, why are you here? I can tell you there is nothing wrong with you. You just need to learn to meditate."*

Her words stunned me. Not because I resisted them, but because they cut through everything else. She had assessed me in her own way, seen through the layers of my narrative, and arrived at a disarmingly simple truth. There was no grand diagnosis, no dire proclamation. Just an invitation: learn to meditate.

I felt no resistance. In fact, I felt relief. Her reputation was solid, her reviews strong, and her firm demeanor carried compassion beneath it. For the first time in a long while, I felt like maybe I wasn't broken. Maybe I just needed to reframe my relationship with my mind.

From the second session onward, she introduced structure. She handed me a packet of papers: office policies, fees, and, most importantly, a set of ten questions. She asked me to answer them wholeheartedly and return them the next week. It was homework, and it demanded honesty.

But the true gift of those sessions came in the final thirty minutes. That was when she guided me into meditation. She showed me the method of completely silencing the mind's continuous chatter, creating a gap between thoughts, and bringing in stillness through breath.

Occasionally, she would have Sanskrit chanting playing in the background. At first, they were strange-sounding, even weird. I didn't know the language, nor did I know the culture they were coming from. But as I kept hearing them, something changed. They became familiar and soothing. I discovered they were prayers, chanting of gods, and holy rites handed down from one generation to another.

I yearned for them more as each week passed. In fact, I not only memorized one chant, the Gayatri Mantra, but I could recite *Om Bhur Bhuva Swaha* perfectly without any mistake, and the sound could be heard as if it were coming from my tongue. Later on, I found out when one should chant it, how it was in harmony with the day's different rhythms, and how its vibrations were like healing something within my being.

I always left her office feeling a sense of relief and inspiration. It was a time of catharsis for me, as if a heavy weight was taken off, not forever, but sufficiently for me to have the space to breathe. I found that I was regularly leaving with a renewed sense of purpose, which often translated into a strong desire for physical activity. The difference between the motel's heaviness and the calm that I took from her office was very noticeable. My third session unlocked something, and the first sign was how often I found myself smiling.

The smiles weren't forced, but were an honest, uninhibited reaction. I find it clear that many people lack the capacity for grace when faced with the unexpected.

Dr. Andersen was definitely one of those people. She was not giving her wisdom in a complicated way. Instead, she simply pointed out how I was thinking badly about myself and pushed me toward the truth. She took away my doubts that were going in circles with the help of her words of power, positivity, and authenticity.

I really felt like her advice was precious. During the three weeks of the sessions, she was a constant reminder of my true self. She equipped me with the means to stop my despair cycles, change how I saw my situations, and be anchored in something stronger than fear.

There were indeed some funny moments, too. I recall times when friends would gather, venting about their husbands, sharing frustrations. I'd find myself repeating Dr. Andersen's phrases, offering reframed perspectives, and inserting little nuggets of wisdom I had just learned. My friends would laugh, sometimes staring at me like I had sprouted a second head.

"Geez, Kath," they joked. "You should be a therapist."

They had no idea I was sneaking Dr. Andersen's influence into those conversations.

What shifted most profoundly was my ability to receive. Before, I resisted help, trying to carry everything alone. But as I continued these sessions, I began to soften.

My heart opened, little by little. I started to view my life as a blank canvas rather than a wreck. Whether it was in the form of encouraging words, helpful advice, or just being there, I was grateful for any support.

Triggers persisted, times when recollections of the past threatened to drag me down. However, they didn't hold me as firmly as they used to. Gradually, their hold relaxed, and the emotions associated with them started to fade.

Looking back, I can see that something within me continued to move forward even during the most trying periods. I got up and did the next little thing, even when I wanted to give up completely. I didn't realize what it was at the time.

I can see now, though, that it was trust. Trust that things would eventually be okay. Trust that I could re-emerge from the wreckage of my experiences. Trust that grace, in its work clothes, would show up right when I needed it.

Chapter 7:
Learning to See What Was Already There

Gratitude was not something that came into my life with loud celebrations. It snuck quietly and in very small ways. When I thought I was going to run out of food, there was a warm meal waiting for me. A safe place to sleep was there, although it was only for a short time.

Someone listened to me without judging me. These were little bits of mercy appearing in very normal things. At times when everything was uncertain, these small things reminded me that I was still being loved in ways I had not seen before.

My days during that time slowly changed, and I had different teachers, the ones I did not expect. I started watching more and more public television. It was not for fun, but to calm my mind. Dr. Wayne Dyer was the person I felt most attracted to. His presence on PBS and YouTube was like a lifeline for me.

His voice, although very calm, was still very powerful and the source of my courage when everything was uncertain. While others viewed religious programs, Dr. Dyer was my church. I never missed a show.

Iyanla Vanzant came next with her passionate energy and no-nonsense kind of speech, which I was really drawn to. I only saw her first as a guest in a popular show - a lawyer turned spiritual coach who made a point in speaking most boldly, especially to women.

What she said was compassionate and powerful, awakening something in me. I eagerly read her works, especially *One Day My*

Soul Opened Up. The book was her way of teaching me that I had to say what I thought and not fear my own truth.

Along with it, I also came across Esther Hicks on YouTube. She was a channel for the spiritual teachings of a higher entity called Abraham. Her talks on the law of attraction and being *"in the vortex"* reassured me that I was not alone. I started to realize that being here and now with my full attention could, in fact, be the cause of the very events and people I wanted to have in my life.

What she said was like an aid to me - as if I were connecting to a higher frequency where life was logical again.

All these teachers gave me something different, but it was Dr. Dyer's message that I remembered the most. His book *The Power of Intention* literally did a 180 in the way I looked at things. He talked about us all plugging into a universal energy source to create the life we most want, making us aware that the Source is always there for us. *"Quieting the mind to hear with the heart is all it takes,"* he said.

One of his phrases that really stuck with me was, *"Give up your personal history; live your life more fully in the present,"* which I found myself repeating over and over, and that really helped me when things were uncertain.

I liked and valued all of their teachings, but they were different in that each connected with a different side of me. From Dr. Dyer, I got the lesson of peace. Iyanla gave me courage. Esther taught me to have faith in what I couldn't see. The three of them, little by little, pulled me out of the pit of despair and into hope.

I looked at life differently because of their teachings. I became mindful of the changes taking place in me, which were more subtle: I was breathing deeper, sleeping better, smiling more often. I felt safe in my own body. There was no pretending, no forced positivity; I've never been one to fake emotions.

Even when I was a little girl, my mother would tell me that I was a terrible pretender because I was so transparent with my feelings. I always spoke the truth, kindly but directly. That honesty has always been with me.

Gratitude, as far as I am concerned, was not about putting on a mask and pretending that everything was alright; it was about acknowledging that there was still something good even when things were bad.

I sincerely think that gratitude should be practiced as an everyday habit. No matter how life treats us, there is always a treasure – a lesson waiting to be uncovered. To be honest, when I started to read and listen more carefully to these spiritual teachers, my view was totally different.

Difficulty, to be more exact, stopped feeling like a punishment and started to look like a personal growth opportunity. I was reading, meditating every day, and noticing that life was becoming less and less difficult. I didn't view difficulties as something to be afraid of; I viewed them as challenges to be solved.

When there was no one to share these discoveries with me, I didn't experience loneliness. I was happy to learn by myself, thankful for the books, PBS, and infinite wisdom available on YouTube, and it always seemed to be there when I was in need.

The memory of this one-car incident is still very clear to me.

So, my car decided to quit on me. Just done.

And the repair bill?

Way beyond what my wallet was willing to negotiate. For a minute, I just sat there, staring into the kind of silence that makes you question every life choice leading up to this point.

Now, the old me? She would've slapped on a *"I've got this"* attitude, pretended everything was under control, and quietly drowned in the problem. But something shifted. This time, I swallowed my pride, called up my mechanic, and laid it out straight: I couldn't afford it.

Guess what?

He didn't judge, didn't lecture. He just said he'd handle it for free, and I'd only need to pay for the parts. It turns out that a little honesty can get you further than all the ego in the world.

The kindness of his action was so unexpected that it was definitely one of the moments when Jesus, the son of God, was disguised as a workman – grace was most at work. Basically, the breaking of the car experience was a lesson to me: if we are people who show our vulnerability and are honest, then help will come to us and not pity.

Gratitude was really my savior at that time when everything was coming apart around me, because instead of sinking into a spiral of despair, it gave me a quiet confirmation: I am taken care of.

I discovered that gratitude was not merely a practice of the spirit, but also a tool for survival. It was the one that kept me down to earth when everything else in my life was changing. Also, I do not stop learning about myself through it even now.

I have become a grateful person, and the first thing that comes to my mind is to thank God for the blessings already here. Indeed, the warmth of a kind word. The steady rhythm of breath.

The invisible hand of grace guides me forward, one quiet moment at a time.

Chapter 8:
Something Bigger
Than My Problems

Faith has always been part of my life, but I think a person only really gets the concept of faith when they don't have anything else to cling to. Having faith also comes with trust that everything is going to work out. I never knew when life would shift; a year after that event happened, life just happened.

Belief shifted to a more positive place, and I was somewhere different before I knew it. Events happened so fast, but as I went through the experience, it felt like I was in it for years. Looking back, I realize that life flowed; I just had to keep going.

I knew not to stop meditating as I found inner peace. Meditation didn't feel like a chore that I had to do. I found ways to make it work out for me. I found myself meditating while going for a walk or even while eating breakfast. The feeling of gratitude strengthened as I engaged in physical activities, cooked, and took care of myself.

Personally, I realized the peace within. These days, it doesn't take hours to be in a meditative zone; it's almost the blink of an eye to get to the feelings of bliss.

Over time, I began to see patterns in everything that had once felt random. When I worked at corporate healthcare, I honestly always doubted that I would end up retiring in the medical field. There was this nagging feeling the whole time, but I couldn't figure it out then.

Many times in the past, before that dark event in my life occurred, I would apply for a job, get the job, and get paid well. However, some event would happen, where I would either be laid off or quit the job for whatever reason. I didn't realize I was being pulled away for a bigger purpose.

My career in the corporate medical field just never took off, and I knew about it; I just didn't know where I was being led to.

Sometimes, when we don't listen to the big signs from spirit, they bring us a bigger sign to go a different direction in life. My so-called "dark night" was that big sign. Perhaps the medical field was not what I signed up to do on this planet.

Through this transformation, my heart softened. There was less and less judgment of others, more and more compassion, no matter what people do, which sometimes makes me want to swat their heads into consciousness.

I have learned to love myself more and take better care of myself. I know I cannot give to others if my cup isn't full. That was my problem last time. I gave, and I was always depleted. I have learned so much from that experience, and I have learned to love that experience as mine.

That was specifically for me. We will all have our own awakening experiences that will be special for us. Mine was so precious that I didn't want to open up to people unless I needed a hand, but it was mine to experience.

My awakening also deepened my sensitivity to the world around me. I have become more and more sensitive to catastrophes. My day-to-day consists of schedules and appointments, and then I would be given impressions and visions about fires, or I would hear and see gunshots, or I would see catastrophic events happen in the U.S. or any part of the world.

Once in a dream, I saw a variety of sea creatures on the beach, and they were washed off. In the news, I saw that this happened in the UK. I sobbed for these creatures when I saw the news. And there were the times when I would suddenly cry for no reason - my day would seem completely normal, nothing to make me sad, and later I would see in the news that Queen Elizabeth had passed away.

There were more events like these, and they became increasingly apparent.

So I began questioning the universe: What am I supposed to do with these visions?

But this connection wasn't new. From a very young age, I felt I didn't belong here. I wanted to go back to the stars. I felt lonely, frowned, and cried a lot as a child. I felt more and saw more than other kids; one might think it was all made up.

But it wasn't.

I knew more about people. I just thought people had the same visions or perceptions. I thought everyone could see lights flickering or colors or sounds around people.

These experiences were never spoken of because I remember stating opinions around people, and I was made fun of. The things I knew about others became my secrets. I kept it to myself.

After completing my sessions with Dr. Andersen, I saw an ad about a lady giving discounts for a facial. I booked a facial with her; her name is Debra. I think meeting her was when I felt my path was laid out for me. Debra is a healer; she lives in the Foothills in San Jose.

She had a great 360-degree view of the Valley. At my facial appointment, I felt her magnetic presence. She only used organic products. The scents that surrounded the room were beautiful. After my session, she gave me an Angel Card Reading, which I had never had before.

Her messages were on point. She and I have become good friends to this day.

Meeting her solidified a path for me to develop my intuitive abilities and to learn to direct my sensitivities to a more grounded and balanced outlet. I sought out a teacher to develop properly, and I have taken many intuitive and mediumship courses and energy medicine since.

I have so many stories, but one that sticks out like a sore thumb was one of the very first readings I gave to a young girl. She was battling a rare disease, and she was only 18. The doctors said she would likely only live into her twenties.

The messages that I received were far different from what she was told. Knowing that I am not a medicine expert, I told her I saw her well beyond her thirties. She currently lives a full life, has graduated from college, and everything.

The second experience was with the first doctor I worked with, who was so generous that they gifted me a year of schooling at the Kerala Ayurveda Academy. When I applied for a job there, I emailed my resume, but I forgot to delete my signature.

My signature says "Psychic Medium" after my name.

After my interview (once I had gotten hired), one of the doctors pulled me aside and asked bluntly, "So, you read people? Do you get messages from spirit?"

I said, "Yes, and I apologize. I forgot to delete my signature."

He made it a point to say, "It's okay. I am a spiritual person."

He asked me if he and his wife were pregnant. They had been trying for a long time to conceive.

On a piece of paper, I wrote "September" and "It's a girl."

Then, some events happened where I didn't hear back from him about the outcomes as I started working at his clinic. Almost four months into my work there, he called me to his office and told me his wife was pregnant and expecting a girl, due in September.

As my path was laid out for me, everything seemed to fall into place, and I was drawn to learning more so that I could help others. One day, life just flowed, and I flowed with it. I worked with the doctors and started seeing clients for private sessions. I got a small place not too far from my work.

Life and Spiritual Coaching felt like a calling because I felt that people need the tools to help them with their day-to-day lives, obstacles, or patterns, coupled with my training in Intuitive Development and Mediumship. I can't help it, but often a client's loved one who had crossed over would come through for them for validation.

They bring uplifting messages to help with the client's situation. Energy Medicine, to help bring a client to a calmer and balanced state.

Looking back, I feel it is with all the connections I have made through this wonderful journey. I cannot pinpoint anyone; they were all instrumental to my successes now. I stay in contact with each of them. I know I will always be doing this work to help others. I am in awe as I reflect on life. I have no words for all the amazing miracles.

These days, I think I find my life meaningful and fulfilling. Life will never be perfect. The obstacles are just events, and I can always change my mind or thoughts to divert things to a more favorable outcome. Some aspects of life aren't within my control, and doing what is best is better. My Corporate Self left my Self many moons ago. I was a totally different person back then. These days, I am calmer about life.

I think healing doesn't happen fully while we are still on this planet, the physical self, maybe, but to be healed means we've reached higher states of awareness. Healers need healing too; we are all healers, we are all intuitive souls.

I learned that this so-called "gift" that people call isn't exclusive to people like me. I had to learn to develop to the point this out to clients properly. Now I can help them develop their innate abilities.

Serving something greater than myself, helping others awaken to their power, has been the most beautiful part of this journey. My life, though imperfect, feels purposeful and whole. There truly is something bigger than my problems, and that something is love, guiding us all home.

Chapter 9:
Rebuilding (With a Different Blueprint)

Life restoration wasn't some snap-your-fingers-and-it's-done kind of deal. It came in slow, like daylight after one seriously long night. Working at the doctor's office pulled me back into rhythm, something solid, something that said, "Hey, you're still standing." Bit by bit, the confidence boosted again. Each paycheck, every bill paid, every small win, all of it was building this quiet kind of stability that I hadn't felt in a long time. After a while, I got my own apartment and even bought a secondhand car.

To be honest, it was not ideal at all. Despite the obstacles, I managed to pull it off. A stack of past-due bills was urgently waiting to be paid. I no longer feel threatened, but instead, I feel joyful knowing that a clearer sign of stronger financial stability is ahead.

Unquestionably, having my own place and waking up to silence instead of noise were things that could not be measured. I made my balcony a little sanctuary of nature and color by decorating it with plants. Sometimes, I would keep myself awake until late, full of innovative business ideas, and at other times, I would allow myself to sleep in on my days off, something I hadn't done for years.

This new concept of stability was quite different, lighter, more liberating, and more alive. It was no longer about accomplishment or perfection. It was about being present. I took my past lessons with humility, viewing those tough years not as errors but as valuable teachers. What I lost had formed me in ways that I could not have learned otherwise. There was freedom in having been broken open and then rebuilt by my own hands.

Success, I realized, wasn't about climbing ladders or impressing others anymore. Instead, it was about surviving the difficult times, being calm when everything around me was chaotic, and having inner peace regardless of the external situation. The real success was internal stability - being aware that my life story didn't define me, but rather what I took from it did. It was about making more good choices, the ones that kept my own well-being intact.

I often laugh about how much my definition of "important" has changed. Once, I would say yes to everything and everyone, even when I was completely drained. At my old 8-to-5 job, I would take on illogical tasks just to keep the peace or prove my value. Now, I look back at that version of myself with kindness, but also with limits. My tone has changed to a more concise way of asking, to where I insist that people consider other options before asking me. I have discovered the strength of the word "no." I have turned into my own caretaker.

Even the change is evident with my clients. They were the ones who used to control my schedule, demanding times that suited only them. Now, however, I am resolute about my working hours, as I know that being true to my own time is an expression of my self-respect. It is not selfishness; rather, it is equilibrium.

Gratitude has become my mode of existence. Each day, I thank the sun for a new day.

I have a daily meditative ritual of facing the east, where the sun rises, to talk with the creator or God, if you will, and engage in meditative prayers expressing gratitude for a new day and asking for protection. During sunset, I face the west, where the sun sets, and once again say my prayers of gratitude as I go through the events of my day.

I have become skilled at being thankful for the little things, the things that most people would walk past without even glancing at them. A hot shower after a tiring day, a soft bed, a quiet morning; these are not just things, they are small but very quiet miracles. And at times, I would find a feather on the ground. A powerful synchronicity reminding me there is something bigger happening, and I am part of a shared experience. When a new client calls me, I respond with a smile and thank them.

Doing my daily self-check-in with my physical body in meditation, where I focus on all my organs, but most particularly my major organs - tuning in and sensing what each organ may need. Listening intuitively to what I feel I can do to improve my health through food. Getting to know what foods help my body rejuvenate and, most of all, heal. Gratitude is no longer a list that I go through; it is a continuous conversation with life.

When trouble comes, it is not that they have the power to make me as unhappy as they were before. I see them as being less significant in some respects, and, moreover, I feel that I am able to handle them better. I have developed my serenity, my recognition that some things will be under my control and some will not. Gratitude is still giving me a very comfortable place to stay in both situations. I firmly believe that I will be able to make the best decisions, not only for me but for others as well.

I have come to learn that plenty is not about money or material things, but rather it is a mental state or a decision to keep calm and have trust. Abundance can be very loving and simple in its manifestation. For example, a friend offering to pay for your meal, a small and cheap but beautiful thing from a thrift shop, or coming across the perfect thing for my home while scrolling through an online marketplace. These little gifts from life's generosity make me very happy.

My increasingly reliable inner compass consistently points me toward the right people and opportunities. I realize that it is way simpler to obey that inner voice when my mind is serene and my heart receptive. I do not claim it; rather, it is my work and everyday interactions where I naturally share my wisdom, not as a show, but as a quiet offering. I listen to others with empathy and thus create the kind of places where they feel safe and recognized. The warmth and honesty of my talks have been a refuge for people to feel safe and loved.

Currently, nothing in my life is taken for granted. One of those instances, which I still cannot wrap my head around, is when I am driving my car; it is almost as if the moment when I sit in the driver's seat and take hold of the steering wheel is like a miracle every time. I used to think about it so much that, after some time, I no longer even thought of the bus or the VTA, and I was so terrified of my safety that I asked myself repeatedly how I could get home if it rained. I see that now, sometimes people do not have a better choice than public transportation. I often feel bad for the people taking that long walk to transit stations, especially in unfavorable weather. I was there once, and it remains a constant reminder for me to always be thankful and to bless people around me. With every step, I seek to act with humility and a compassionate heart.

I constantly remind myself of how far I have come from those difficult times, which, by the way, are everywhere: my cozy little apartment in the city, my ability to walk to the local shops, and the peace of mind that comes with the freedom to spend a little extra without fear. What I came to realize is that freedom is not just money-related; it spans over the emotions, spirit, and, basically, humanity.

If I were allowed to convey only one message to people reshaping their lives after grief, it definitely would have been this one: Actively nurture a sense of peace within yourself, and don't forget to breathe. You're not abandoned. When things get difficult, keep your heart open to support and guidance. Be willing to accept the changes that come. Moreover, always, always keep taking care of your body, have your meals, follow your water consumption, and be a source of strength to your heart. The body holds the memory of affection and is quick to respond when properly nurtured. In the end, healing is not a place to which one arrives. It is a slow and gentle way back to oneself.

Chapter 10:
The Call to Share
What I'd Learned

It really seems like that time was only yesterday. It's actually true that I didn't even realize how much time had passed from my very first session with a client, but I still keep that memory in my mind like it was frozen in a special way; not more than a handful of really transformative moments can be crystallized like that. The thing is, before getting here, with all that had happened, the loss, the getting back of what was lost, my slow return to my own self, I used to think, well, I don't think that I have that much to lose. Essentially, I was already playing as if I had the part, although I was not aware that this jump would become the most significant work of my life.

2007 was the year I started living a double life, as I continued my corporate job while also taking on part-time spiritual guidance. I didn't charge clients in those days; I would see them on weekends and sometimes in the evenings if it was over the phone. My old 8-to-5 job at the office was full of tasks that didn't make sense but which I would take on just to keep the peace or demonstrate my worth, and I was always conforming to someone else's expectations. Nevertheless, this work, to be called and be the one who helps others to find their spiritual paths and regain their clarity in their most difficult moments, was completely different. It was the only thing that ever felt right, as if all the pieces of my life that were broken had been there to make up one thing.

As of 2010, I was already making up my mind that it would be the time for a real leap of faith. It was time to let the people know about this work, to fully own it. That was the year I acquired a business license and the insurance needed to run a legitimate business. I remember seeing my first official client at a local park as I worked on establishing myself as a business owner. I couldn't afford the cost to rent an office space just yet, but I thought seeing clients at a cozy, well-maintained park where dogs weren't allowed was actually a beautiful alternative. Something was healing about being surrounded by nature, by open sky and fresh air.

I digress, prior to meeting with my first client, I went all out and advertised with what was then Amazon Local, a platform where local business owners were highlighted and promoted. People would book sessions at a discounted rate, and Amazon Local would take its cut from the sales. This way, the client sessions were prepaid. Clients would then call to make an appointment. When the ads came out, I managed to book a full calendar. The response was a mixture of both excitement and fear. It was amazing to see that people were actually coming to me for what I had to offer.

I still can't get the memory of my first client out of my head. It was a moment that changed my life just as much as it changed hers. The client was a little girl who came to see me with her mother. At that time, she was only seventeen. I remember that she was wearing dark clothes, and her face looked very pale, with her nails painted black – it seemed like a kind of uniform for a person trying to find her identity among the shadows. Her mother, after seeing that her daughter needed no further explanations, left her with me. I was very nervous. Maybe it was her appearance that made me think in this way, but she had a very loving heart. She was extremely and sincerely interested in spirituality, searching for something real in a world that was maybe too much for her.

In her own words, the reading I gave her was "transformative". She came prepared with questions and left the session with a deep feeling of relief. She was acknowledged, as though someone had finally understood her and given her the way and the light that she had been seeking. Her name is Maiah, and even after all these years, I not only see her as a client but also as a friend. Her mom and her grandmother have come to me for sessions as well. The ripple effect of that first meeting still moves through my life.

Just like the majority of my clients, they were genuinely baffled by the validations they received from their higher frequency guidance or spirit. When something resonates that deeply, when the messages land with that kind of precision, people know they've encountered something real. They then refer their family members to see me for sessions, creating these beautiful webs of connection. During my session with Maiah, I had an epiphany of such clarity that you could say it was the moment when my life's purpose finally revealed itself to me. Yes, each day ever since has been like a constant reaffirmation of this fact. Apart from my life as a licensed realtor, I consider my office to be my creative hub.

This work goes beyond the mere provision of guidance; it entails, as I understand it, the somewhat spiritual act of 'holding the sacred space' for people's pain, the questions they can't help but throw at the walls, and their deep longing for clarity and purpose. And to link it to the past, it seems that everything I have experienced, in particular, every devastating blow, every moment of despair, and even those difficult lessons that I have had to earn through struggle, has all been my training for this very moment.

Through the power of retrospection, I came to realize that this calling is mine, even though it emerged during the darkest years of my early childhood. Even then, I somehow knew and believed I was blessed with a unique gift—the ability to see colors around people. To me, it was obvious that many things about people and places, which those around me dismissed as imagination or fabrication, were true.

As for my childhood, I was very much extroverted, and at the same time, I was tuned into the same frequencies that the majority of the world simply can't perceive. I felt and saw that which many kids and people didn't see or feel. Through some sort of divine magic, I had always known that if you listen all the while being still and take in the silence of what is being spoken. I had taken lessons in breathing, and more to that, I had made it my habit of always questioning the thoughts that popped into my head: *Are they really mine, are they messages, or just plain noise?*

Nevertheless, the areas to which I was sensitive in my environment still required proper handling, polishing, and understanding. I did go through a lot of spiritual training with one of the world's leading esoteric teachers in order to better my emotions and, perhaps more importantly, to acquire the skill of discernment, the know-how of telling the difference between intuition and projection, between guidance and fear. Life somehow brought me teachers exactly when I needed them.

After the meetings with Dr. Andersen, I felt a strong pull toward energy medicine. Shortly after, I was drawn to take mediumship certification courses, then life and spiritual coaching, and many more courses in the holistic healing and spiritual industry. The learning just snowballed, each course opening doors to the next. What I have learned and currently apply in my own life has become the very tool I bring forth to help my clients. I wasn't teaching theory; I was sharing what had actually worked to save and transform my own life.

As my practice began to take shape, I held onto a saying that resonated deeply with me: *"If you build it, they will come."* I believed in that philosophy, making continuous improvements one step at a time, not rushing to create a big, flashy practice by spending a lot of money on advertising. The majority of my clients came from organic sources. They were mostly referred to me by other satisfied clients, which felt like the highest compliment. Word of mouth, built on trust and real results, became my foundation.

When I first started, I did harbor fears about how the world would view my work. Would people think I was a fraud? Would they dismiss what I did as nonsense? But those fears lasted only for a short time, and that's because I took the initiative to reach out to many others in the holistic, spiritual, and coaching fields. Many of the people I met who were in the same trade had similar views and some remarkably similar life experiences. I didn't feel alone anymore. I had found my tribe.

After seeing clients at the park, I transitioned to working from home, and then shortly after, I was able to rent an office space, a real, dedicated healing space that felt like a dream come true. To date, I currently see clients around the world, and remarkably, the clients who came in for sessions the first time many years ago are still my clients. Many of them have moved to different U.S. states and countries, yet they continue to book sessions with me. I have made so many friends and now have extended families, clients who became friends and now have claimed me as theirs, and I have done the same. These relationships sustain me.

My clients are very different from one another; they have different backgrounds and different belief systems. However, the main issues that almost always lead them to my office are relationship problems and the search for their purpose – these two fundamental human questions: How do I love and be loved? And what am I here to do? It often happens that I see them for a relationship issue, and the next time, it's something completely different. Life keeps throwing new challenges at us, new growth opportunities.

I have met a vast number of people who seek guidance and understanding, and at the same time feel lost in their own lives. I see people coming to me after a distressing experience; they are carrying with them sorrow, confusion, and a desperate hope. While I set a safe place for them, hear them, and assure them that they are safe and can let their emotions go without being judged, it can be a little hard at times.

Sometimes it is difficult to bear the burden of other people's pain. Nevertheless, I know that my work is to be there, listen without judging, give them the true and genuine messages, and make them realize that they are the ones who can choose their lives. They are not the ones who want me to fix them, but to help them remember their own power; that is what they really need.

It is vital for me to set up the right atmosphere for a good conversation before my sessions and to have good boundaries, which are essential practices, and these are the instruments that I can also show to my clients. Boundaries are not barriers; they are the framework that allows true familiarity and healing to take place in a safe way.

One of the main methods I use is to show people how to dismantle the mental concepts they have created. These are the stories that we tell ourselves, which eventually become our prisons. I get them to verbalize their problems neutrally in my office, where they can actually see themselves talking. Then I have them say their sentences again, and we analyze together what they have just said. Quite frequently, they realize that their feelings were unnecessarily intensified, that they were reacting to a story rather than to the facts. So, it becomes our task to reframe those sentences, uttering them again, but this time using words and expressions that are consistent with their inner self. The point is to be truthful to oneself without dramatizing one's stories beyond what they actually are.

The work required specific tools and practices that became central to my coaching, techniques I had gathered from many teachers along the way. I got involved in many spiritual groups over the years. I used to go to this non-denominational church where I attended and participated in so many activities. One gathering that I attended most faithfully was the Oneness Blessings, which was often paired with singing bowl meditations and sound baths. I gave Deeksha, and I attended these gatherings every Sunday evening, finding community and practice in equal measure. The group engaged in chants and affirmations to cleanse each Chakra center, and one that particularly resonated with me was the "I AM LOVE" chant. We would repeat "I AM LOVE" for seven minutes, and at that point, the words were not merely sounds; they were the truth resonating with every cell.

Writing down my thoughts and meditation exercises significantly improved my relationship with myself, uncovering more of the inner self that I was not aware of. These were the very same practices that I would introduce to my clients, not as far-off concepts they should try, but as real experiences that had been my way through the dark times. I hadn't realized, but I knew very well what it was like to be with your own darkness, to confront the patterns that were no longer good for you, because I had gone through that tough, wonderful process all alone. Every tool I offered came from a place of hard-won understanding, not from theory in a textbook.

As I continue this work to help clients and people I encounter, I can see myself reflected in their suffering. Their difficulties reflect fragments of my own path, and now I have a better understanding, which has raised my compassion for them. I often get these moments of deep gratitude, almost being overwhelmed by how far I have come.

I still cannot figure out how I could have made it without the people who were there for me during my darkest hours. Sometimes, small fragments of their lives reflect my past experiences and thus bring back the old pain or the old victories. However, the manner in which they deal with their own narratives will always be their choice, and I am not able to compare their stories with mine.

Our tales, being different, beautiful, and special, deserve to be recognized separately. I am fond of my narrative; it has the power to bring me back to my core, reminding me of what is achievable if you are determined not to give up.

My clients telling me what has happened since I saw them last is always, to me, a source of great uplift. I delight in knowing that they are making the changes through the means I have offered and that they have grown. I have always kept my doors open to my clients in this way. I love visiting with them or receiving an unexpected call from them wanting to talk with me, just to thank me or to leave me a five-star review. Every person I help completes another layer of my own healing journey, creating this beautiful, ongoing cycle of service and continued growth. Their victories remind me of how far I've come, and their struggles remind me to stay humble and grateful, to never forget where I started.

Honestly, I do not see myself stepping down anytime soon. This is the field I truly love; therefore, I will continue serving people as long as I have the capacity. What I live for has expanded beyond what I could have ever anticipated, especially when I was going through those rough days full of despair and uncertainty. I can't wait to share more of my creativity with the world because it really brings me joy, and I love sharing it with others.

I got myself into the trap of painting, and now I have quite a few pieces on canvas. I produce candles and bath soaps, and I do not forget to bring in intention and care in every single one of my creations. I am even considering launching a store in 2026, a real-life place where people can come and experience the beauty and healing that I am committed to providing. I keep changing, and I am over the moon that I decided to be born in this lifetime at this very moment.

Actually, it is only now that I recall that all those rough times, the moments when I was broken, and the lessons that I learned the hard way were the things that made me ready for this mission. The years of struggle were not thrown away or without a reason; in fact, they were necessary.

They made me very compassionate, which no book or course or comfortable life could have ever done. They gave me the insight that one can only get by going through fire and making the decision to rebuild again and again. So, nowadays, every time I meet with a client, every time I support someone who is going through pain and sees a way out, I am reminded that the deepest scars in our lives, if we decide to turn them into wisdom and give that wisdom to the people who need it most, can become our greatest gifts. This is the work. This is the calling. And I wouldn't trade it for anything.

Chapter 11:
Tools That Actually Work (When You're Barely Hanging On)

People often ask me what it was that saved my life in those terrible times, and they expect me to tell them about some huge epiphany or an astonishing intervention. The reality is much simpler, and I would say more viable. What essentially saved me were the small, repeatable, and controllable actions that I could still do even when I was close to breaking down. They were not theoretical ideas taken from books that I had to verify through practice, but rather lived experiences in which, stripped down to nothing, it seemed that going out of bed was the most challenging thing in the world, and the situational heaviness was on the verge of crushing me completely.

Gratitude was what literally kept me alive, but not in the typical way people refer to it. I definitely don't mean it as a form of positive thinking done by force or pretending that everything was fine when it clearly wasn't. What I mean is dig through the impenetrable darkness to find the tiniest pieces of light, and make it a habit to spot them even though at every turn you find that there is nothing to be thankful for.

The custom had quite a modest beginning; it was simply a question of necessity. Regardless of the weather, I had started to wake up every morning to the sound of birds singing outside my window, my body deeply relaxed and lying comfortably in bed. In those very first moments of waking up, before the heaviness of my reality would fall on me again, I let myself recognize that it was indeed very comforting to be there at that moment. I would give thanks to life with a smile, as a whole, and to my good health without a word. It sounds as if it were too simple, doesn't it? But at the time of barely surviving, simple is exactly what saves you.

During the whole day, I kept catching myself being grateful for anything and everything. A warm bagel. My protection. The fact that I was safe in that moment. This practice somehow became automatic, woven into the fabric of my existence without effort. I didn't have to force it anymore; my mind had been retrained to seek out these moments of grace.

Hiking became another powerful gratitude practice. Being surrounded by the beauty of nature, breathing in the fresh air, and taking in new scenery, these experiences brought me back to myself. They reminded me that the world was larger than my pain, that beauty existed even when I couldn't feel it inside myself. These small acts of gratitude brought me a deeper perspective on life and cultivated compassion for others who might be less fortunate than I am.

I often found myself wondering about people who didn't even have what I had. How did their night go? With all the prevalent homelessness I saw around me, I knew many were unhoused, many who had acquired higher education and were still unable to afford a place to rent or meet their basic needs. This realization changed my inner world. I started to do things like playing a part in the food bank, in which I donated to the organization, and also organizing a coat drive for the homeless in the cold and rainy seasons. My own hard times had opened my heart to other people's, and by that opening, I discovered my purpose.

However, gratitude was not enough by itself. I also needed to confront the things I had been avoiding for years. The thing I am now calling shadow work – at that time, I was not familiar with the term. I only knew that there were parts of my personality that I was neglecting, incidents that I had been hiding, and patterns that I was repeating without knowing the reason.

After many times of ignoring a painful event, life will not allow you to indefinitely avoid shadow work, as I see it. When a difficult experience has happened and is not taken into consideration for the first few times, the next time will come when another painful incident occurs that provokes those parts of ourselves that have been deeply buried for many years. As an illustration, if a person is in an unhealthy relationship where he/she is subjected to verbal, mental, and emotional abuse, he/she may search for means of improvement or ways to hide or cover up the painful incidents without actually resolving them. That person might allow the same volatile behavior to be directed at them day after day, year after year, thus creating a false sense of calm, although the relationship is abusive.

Nevertheless, through the difficult times, life, in its wise way, offers us opportunities to defend ourselves, shows us that there is a way out of challenging situations, and, what is even more important, helps us discover our value. The universe knows we have the potential to be more than we think, and it brings us, sometimes through painful experiences, the opportunities to learn to love and respect ourselves and to say no to abuse.

When I went through those times of deep and devastating helplessness, it was in some way clear to me that nobody else would come and rescue me but me alone. I made time for myself, I practiced what I call "self-talk", and I was a listener to myself, a listener to my body, which was responding to the words I uttered. I trained myself to use gentle words to myself and to trust that no matter what, everything would turn out fine. It would be me; that is fine.

One of the most empowering activities that came into my life is mirror work, which I got hold of the knowledge of through one of my mentors. It's a technique whereby a person, standing in front of a big mirror, is looking at him/herself with love and is either talking silently or aloud, just like chatting with a close friend. The person utters words such as "Hi! You're courageous! You really did well today. I'm grateful to you for showing up. You're looking great. You have the most beautiful smile."

At first, doing such work seemed like a joke. I couldn't even see myself in the eye without feeling shame and disgust. Nevertheless, I kept coming back; I kept confronting that mirror, although I really wanted to leave. The change took place slowly. I started to judge myself less and even to feel pity for myself instead of shame. The things I said became increasingly accurate.

I used a mirror to speak to my inner child, and, surprisingly, it turned out to be one of the most powerful healing exercises I've come across. It brought on a surge of childhood memories, allowing me to trace certain behaviors straight back to their origins. It didn't stop at childhood alone; it brought back the good moments, the mischievous version of me, and the sad ones I preferred leaving in storage. It also gave me the chance to see my coping mechanisms for what they were, how I tried to protect myself when I watched my parents fight, and to finally notice the patterns that had been running my life without my awareness.

In doing so, I was able to speak to my inner child more calmly, telling her she mattered and that the pressure my parents put on me to do better in school, usually mixed with frustration, had nothing to do with her worth. And, credit where it's due, I thanked my parents, because they were the ones who made those difficult school years bearable by bringing in tutors.

This practice helped me heal repressed parts of myself and uncomfortable emotions. It developed self-love and allowed me to accept and understand my behaviors and to integrate the parts of myself that I'd deemed unfavorable. It is continuous work that never really ends.

Journaling was another essential tool. I have stacks of journals from those years. It was through writing that I found an outlet for my emotions, as they fell either on the good side or the heavy side. Even on the days when I didn't want to write, I did, as it was a kind of pressure valve that released additional energy. At other times, I was doodling so that the words would flow. I also used to ask myself what it would be like to create stories that could capture a reader's interest, and I wanted to become an author one day. And now, at this moment, I get to tell you my story.

These practices have helped me notice the patterns that I kept repeating. I went with fear on my shoulder, but the pretense was that all was well. My mind would put itself into an escape mode at any given time. The fact that I received a letter triggered a great level of anxiety to the point that I did not feel like opening it. That response would always give me a shock of fear.

The trick that I found to notice this pattern was paying attention, or being there with my own reactions. As time went by, I found breath work to be effective, and the issues that I had blown out of proportion in my mind were often not as large as I thought. Breath work became my core practice, the one I held onto when fear threatened to unbalance me.

I already knew that a new beginning of my life would be long and hard, yet I was prepared to face it. I also had to confront things alone, and there were times when I would feel like giving up due to the weight. In those moments of despair, amidst the waves of powerlessness, there were also moments when I seemed to think that all was turning to ashes, and the darker thoughts were tempting me to sink into the depths. Yet, even then, I did not stop making my way toward the light that remained.

What kept me going? Taking the courage to wake up and start each day again. Doing what I could. Asking for strength. Dreaming bigger than my circumstances. Applying all the wonderful resources and tools that I was taught by my mentors. They equipped me for this journey. They gave me wisdom, support, and most of all, love.

Finding those teachers and that guidance was essential. I am a very enthusiastic reader and enjoy conducting deep research. I have been fascinated by self-help books throughout my life. Back when Kindles were a luxury, I'd often visit the local Barnes & Noble with very little money. Books on self-motivation and empowerment were numerous and written by reputable authors.

An example is *The Power of Now* by Eckhart Tolle, which was a great turning point in my life since it is a book that does not focus on anything in the past or even on what should happen in the future, but it focuses on the present moment. I was in complete agreement with this book since most of the things that were discussed by the author are the ones that I have personally discovered as a result of my personal experience. That book was an affirmation that the way my mind worked was correct, that I wasn't insane for my way of thinking.

I used to consider my instructors as spiritual teachers, yet mostly I have learned and grown through books. Some wisdom, too, came from movies such as "The Secret". The movie was a turning point for me in understanding the laws of the universe, especially the law of attraction and manifestation. Once again, this movie was instrumental in my thinking of going beyond what the mind thought was possible and not being limited by thoughts anymore. I loved the idea of expansion, of becoming more than my circumstances.

Guidance also came in unexpected forms. A stranger's kindness on a difficult day. A line from a song that landed exactly when I needed to hear it. The way sunlight fell through the trees on a particularly dark morning. I learned to be open to insight from unexpected sources, to understand that teachers come in different forms when we are ready to learn.

If any of you are feeling stuck or helpless at this moment, I would like to share with you the very thing I wish someone had told me when I was buried in the depths of my struggle. First of all, every person's journey is different and of great value. I took full responsibility for my journey. I even went further to say that I love it because it is mine. Your turn now; take full responsibility for your life, love it, and be eternally thankful for the opportunity to learn to become the best version of yourself, no matter what that looks like.

I would recommend learning what meditation is and its benefits because once we master the art of quieting the mind, it becomes very clear, and we know exactly what to do. Find a teacher who could guide you in that. With all the technology in today's world, many choose to learn online, and you can also find credible apps. Take the first step. If you can hardly sit still for five minutes, don't expect to meditate for an hour. Start right where you are.

Just keep practicing gratitude even when it feels as though you are not able to do so. Look for one thing each day, no matter how small, that you are thankful for. It could be as simple as a warm bed, a cup of coffee, or the fact that you are still breathing. Let that be enough.

Work on the mirror technique even when it is the last thing you want to do, especially when you feel most uncomfortable. Look at yourself in the eye and talk to yourself as if you were talking to someone you love with all your heart. Your inner child is the one who needs to hear those things from you.

Start a journal. Put down words without censoring yourself. Let the emotions be the ink and the page your paper. You don't have to write; rather, you have to be truthful and write.

Learn breathing exercises. When a situation of fear or anxiety is about to take over, come back to your breath. It is always there, ready for you, and free of charge.

And be patient with yourself. There is no end to our own transformation; I see it as a lifelong event. We never stop learning as long as we are on this planet; we are bound to have life experiences. The key is how we choose to handle these life situations.

Healing is a continuous cycle. On the other hand, when a person gains wisdom to the extent that they can share it with others, then they become a teacher. Once you are the teacher, you are obligated to have better control over your emotions, to behave in a way that is consistent with your words, and to actually do the things that you say others should do.

My personal transformation was not a one-day event. It took a very long time and continuous effort, and even when I was not feeling it, I still did it for myself, and I kept on deciding that healing was possible. There were times and situations in which I could only see my old patterns and feel as if all the progress I had made was gone. But anyway, I continued, I was still practicing, and I kept making this choice.

Healing takes longer than we want and is also faster than we are scared of. There will be days when you will be able to see great progress and days when you will feel that you have come back to the very beginning. These are all stages of the process and are important.

The thing I want you to know is the following: the methods that result in success are quite simple; however, they demand that one be consistent. They require that you be there for yourself from day to day, and especially on those days when you are not feeling like it. Also, they require that you believe, even if it is only a little, that you deserve to be put through the effort.

You are the one who deserves to be put through the effort. Time is also yours. Love and compassion, which you would readily give to another, are also yours. Give it to yourself first. Place the first step there. Take small steps on the starting path. But still place the first step.

These resources, including gratitude, shadow work, mirror practice, journaling, breath work, and meditation, were the things that helped me when I was going through the darkest period of my life. They will be the things that help you when you go through your darkest period as well. Not because they are magical, but because they teach you to be present with yourself, to be kind to yourself, and to remember that you are not your circumstances; you are the one who can choose how to respond to them.

Moreover, through the act of choosing to be there for yourself every day, you uncover something truly profound: you are much stronger than you thought, you are more resilient than you had ever imagined, and you have more potential for change than you ever believed.

This was the truth that I found out. That is the truth I offer you now. Take what resonates. Leave what doesn't. But please, keep going. The world needs you whole.

Chapter 12:
Your Story Matters Too
(And You're Not Alone)

If this chapter happens to be the one that you are reading in the middle of your own crisis, I wish I could speak to you directly. I am not the one pretending to have all the answers; I am not the one comfortably on the other side, telling you that it gets better; rather, I am the one who can recall the exact feeling of being in your place.

Among all the essential things that you should never forget is to take care of yourself and treat yourself kindly. I know that this might sound hardly plausible when you are about to break apart, and every day is a struggle with everything that surrounds you. But, at this stage, it is the only thing you can actually do to start there. And even the faintest ray of good amid all that agony, make it be your own. Support yourself so you can have a more meaningful and healthy daily life, perhaps by taking a walk or jog, or by making yourself eat something that refreshes and energizes your body. Such small signs of taking care of yourself are not egocentric, but they are the tools of survival.

Asking someone to assist you also should not be feared. You can find some genuinely good people out there who will support you without making you feel inferior. I understand that reaching out may feel shameful or like you should be able to manage on your own, but needing help is not a failure; it's a natural part of being human. The pain becomes even more terrible if you stay alone. Allow someone to get close to you.

Sometimes, if you want to bring relief to a person, you should listen to them carefully. Most of the time, simply offering support in the presence of the suffering person is a tremendous help to them. It is not always through doing, and I am aware of the fact that people will always recall how we made them feel. I personally am convinced that being present is a powerful thing. Being there with them and being there for them is the way that they will feel that their experience is real and so validated.

If you are the one to be in pain now, please take someone in to be with you. You are not obliged to have all the words. You are not obliged to tell everything in the perfect way. Just let somebody be with you in your pain. Let them bring you food or give you a hand with the errands. These are basic, physical expressions of care that can, at times, keep you alive when you are in enormous trouble.

I want you to know something, which I could not realize until years had passed: you are not the only one. I realize that you may believe that no one can ever know what exactly you are going through at this time in your life. But we are all suffering; we suffer one way or another.

It may be the death of a loved one, loss of employment, accident, or any other form of crushing life event. Pain comes to us in many forms; it is simply part of being human. We are feelers, not machines. Your pain is valid. Your struggle is real. And you are not the only person who has been that way.

People came into my life a few times, only in unexpected situations, without their knowing what I had gone through. I remember that, on some occasions, such cases occurred when I was having the worst thoughts of giving up. Nevertheless, it was ever so that an untimely phone call by a friend who only wanted to chat or visit a cafe would find me. It was during these periods that the bonds of the friendships were the greatest to me, and I knew that I required them in my life.

The relationships we had at the time that kept me alive. Not because my friends told me something profound or that they fixed my problems, but because they helped me realize that I was not the world; I was still a component of something bigger, something that was not my suffering. When I was not in a position to feel it, they made me feel that I mattered.

I have finally come to understand a profound aspect of sharing one's personal struggles: a person's life can become a source of healing for others. A cure in the sense that the person who shares their story and the people who surround them get different views of the difficult sides of life.

Sharing also builds connections, maybe because of the familiarity of life situations. People seem to have a better understanding, and it also breaks down some barriers and judgments.

I navigated through that difficult part of my life in the ways I knew how; no one gets the experience firsthand to be called an expert. There is no such thing. Every struggle is unique and personal for each individual. Sharing life experiences also breaks down the feelings of isolation and shame. It takes being brave to own up to our own personal struggles and loving ourselves in the process. In essence, our struggles teach us to be gentler with ourselves, allowing us to extend that same grace to others.

Let me tell you about someone whose story moved me deeply. She wasn't a client in my coaching practice but a friend who had to flee her country to move to Canada to stay with her extended family, with very little money. She was the oldest child, and she struggled with her family's expectations and judgment of her. She was always belittled and verbally abused and told, "she was never going to amount to anything."

She didn't have a lot of skills. She didn't know how to use a computer. She had not worked many jobs, but she was good with people. She started out as a cleaning lady in Toronto, Canada, and once again endured years of hardship. She had a chance to move to the U.S. on a working visa, again struggling a lot to gain stability.

Until she gained stability, she met an employer from a church that she started attending, and they took a chance on her. She worked for that employer, then went to night school and took courses to become a licensed aesthetician. She was introduced to me by another friend a few years ago. She shared her story with me while I kept mine private.

I think a lot about the strength one must have to be able to recover from tough situations in life. The truth is, the human spirit is very resilient in times of hardship. Occasionally, the thought might even cross our mind that we do not have the strength to carry on yet, and lo and behold, we find the strength we need. These kinds of stories are not only a source of entertainment but also a reminder to make better decisions; we could either decide to quit or to keep going. It also got me thinking: *what would I have done if I had been her?*

Honestly, her narrative healed me in a way that neither downplayed my own pain nor made me feel like I should be more grateful for what I have. It is simply because her story reminds us all of the incredible power within us to change and transform ourselves. The most revealing thing for me was that resilience is not something that you have firmly or strongly; instead, it's something you come to realize when giving up is not an option.

Moreover, I want you to grasp this point: your story is important as well. The one that you are living right now, despite the fact that you are going through a hard time and that the road ahead is not visible. The stories we have are capable of becoming healing agents for other people. Not that you need to have all the solutions or that you have to have completely conquered everything in your life already, but rather that your sincere battle, the fact that you decide to go on in spite of everything, can help someone else find their way when they face a similar situation that is to come.

Yet, the truth remains that you need to get through it first. Even though you are in the middle of your struggle, you still need to seek meaning and transformation in it. It certainly sounds impossible to me as well. When you are going under, you do not think about the lessons that the water drowning you could teach you. Your instinct is simply to gasp for air.

Therefore, I want to share a thought with you: In my opinion, being mindful and accepting the situation without judgment or blame is the first step toward beginning the journey. It would be efficient to start focusing on the desired outcomes, even if doing so is quite difficult, especially when one is completely carried away by emotions. For me, it was very helpful to acknowledge what I was going through; I was not dreaming, it was real.

We sometimes tend to resist change instead of accepting the events as they come and being honest with ourselves. If I were to deny my experience, I would not really know how I would prolong my suffering. I was forced to learn how to escape from the negative thinking cycle, as it was not doing me any good. I was forced to learn how to treat myself kindly and gently, just like how I would treat a loved one. I learnt to choose to focus on what I could control and what I could do to help the situation, and it was really hard.

Work needs to be done, although it is difficult, to see small changes. Try, as a life situation, however difficult, to see it as an opportunity for personal growth, for instance. We can only blossom and grow after we have accepted and forgiven ourselves. It is important to do things that are productive in order to keep ourselves engaged in a positive way.

Journaling is an excellent tool. As we write in our journals, we are helping ourselves with better memory. It lowers the stress levels, enhances the way we regulate our emotions, helps to clarify our thoughts, and, most importantly, helps to identify the old cycles of patterns that we are stuck in. Journaling helps identify those patterns that are outdated.

Look for small signs of light. They won't be dramatic. They won't be obvious. But they'll be there. A moment when the crushing weight lifts just slightly. A day when you realize you smiled without forcing it. A conversation that reminds you that connection is still possible. A small choice you made to care for yourself instead of punishing yourself. These are the glimmers. Notice them. Honor them. Let them be enough for now.

Your capacity for transformation is already within you. It's not something you have to go out and find, purchase, or earn. Maybe it's hard to see because the pain covers it, but the light is there. The light you are looking for is not coming from the outside, but you are the one who emits it from the inside, even when you can't feel it, even when everything seems to be dark.

This change is not a straight road. It's not a direct line from sorrow to recovery. It's a disorder and a complex thing, with regressions and progressions, with days when you feel that you've advanced and days in which you feel that you are at the starting point again. All of this conforms to the rules of the norm. All of that is part of the process.

And let me throw that out for you to think about, even though it may feel like the farthest thing from possible: someday, when you have moved on and are in a different place, you may become the last person someone expects to teach them. It will not necessarily be because it is your duty, or you have to, or it is a requirement, but simply because, at the time of sharing, it can be one of the most healing things you ever do.

Being open to others' judgment is not a sign of being weak but rather a sign of being strong. Improvement of oneself is continual learning as long as humans live on the earth. We are the owners of our experiences and the ways they have taught us to be strong, as well as how they have taught us to treat others.

Always remind yourself of the times that you were able to come through those experiences and what helped you to get through them. How are you today? How do you keep your peace? First of all, be thankful for all the opportunities that come your way. Secondly, be faithful to your own self, speak the truth with love, and do not judge others. Besides that, simply be yourself.

Yet, the question is, how are you going to know that moment when you would want to share your experience with others? If it is your story, then you ought to have felt that you had really processed the anger, bitterness, or resentment that arose from it. Sharing your experience when you are still hurting can be damaging to both you and the people who hear it. The feeling to tell one's story comes from a sense of purpose, not from a feeling of revenge or a need for external validation.

It may be that you want to do it to give others a hand, to be a guide for their change, or simply to say your truth. Question yourself: will you be prepared for people's reaction or criticism to your story? If you indeed feel the intense urge to share your personal experience with people, it would be nice to get support from friends or family members to help you go through the emotions that this may bring.

The moment that a story is told and it doesn't hurt you, but instead it makes you think of the progress you have made, is when you will know that you are ready. You will be aware of the moment when you are able to share as a grounded person and not as someone looking for validation or understanding from others. The very first reason for sharing the story will then be to give hope rather than to talk through one's own painful experience.

But if you are not there yet, it's perfectly fine. That is actually much more than fine. At the moment, the only thing that is required from you is to keep on living through the hard times. To endure. To treat yourself with kindness. To request help. Being conscious of even the most minuscule light rays. Still holding on to faith, even if it is just a tiny bit, that change can happen.

Life is a book that you have not yet finished writing. You are the main character of the story, and it is not necessary for you to know the ending. You do not need to have it all figured out. It's not necessary that you are healed, or complete, or perfect. Simply continuing to be there for yourself is enough, one day at a time, one moment at a time.

It is not your obligation to handle this situation alone. The pain you experience is what makes you one of the people who have suffered, struggled, and doubted their capacity to carry on.

The light will come. Not because I can give you the guarantee that everything will turn out well or that your problems will be solved in the way you want. It's just that you haven't yet discovered your resilience.

You will not stop to surprise your inner strength. Your story matters; it is of value, and when you are ready, it will become the medicine for someone else who will need to hear that survival is possible.

So please don't quit. Take care of yourself. Love yourself as you would love someone else. Support yourself with others. See the sparks. Trust the process even if you can't see the way.

We fool along with each other to get out of our troubles, which are different for each of us; we learn our lessons, and we find our light. And one day, perhaps quicker than you think, you will turn back and see that the worst thing that happened to you gave you your greatest gift: the ability to empathize with the pain of others, to give them hope, and to remind them that they, too, are not alone.

This is the inheritance of suffering changed. This is the drug that we give to each other. This is how we turn our deepest wounds into our deepest wisdom. Not by denying the pain, not by pretending that it didn't hurt, but by going through it fully and coming out the other side with broken hearts, ready to be with others on their own journeys.

Your story is powerful. Continue living your truth and trust in the possibility of change; your current strength is a testament to it.

Reader's Notes

As you close this chapter and reflect on your own journey, take a moment to pause, breathe, and listen to what your heart wants to say. Let the questions below guide your reflection, helping you uncover meaning, clarity, and the quiet wisdom within your experiences.

- Looking back, what moments now feel like part of a "divine setup" that redirected your path?

- How did your transformation change the way you view others - family, friends, or even strangers?

- Were there any experiences that opened your heart or deepened your empathy?

- How has your definition of success changed after everything you have experienced?

- How did your gratitude practice evolve once life became easier again?

- How do you now understand or experience abundance?

About the Author

Katherine Dacanay is a woman whose life was transformed not by circumstance but by faith, surrender, and divine guidance. After walking through one of the most challenging seasons of her life, she experienced a spiritual awakening that reshaped everything she believed about purpose, intuition, and God's timing. What felt like the end became the beginning of her rebirth, a journey that taught her how to slow down, listen deeply, and recognize the Holy Spirit's voice in ways she had never noticed before.

Her story is one of resilience, rediscovery, and radical trust. Through moments of loss, confusion, and emotional exhaustion, Katherine learned to rely on God with a new level of intimacy. She began to see every setback as a "divine setup," every redirection as intentional, and every delay as a form of protection. From this transformation emerged a renewed sense of purpose, to share her testimony, to encourage others, and to remind people that healing and abundance are possible no matter where they begin.

In her daily life, Katherine practices gratitude as a way of living, not as a checklist. She has learned to appreciate the sacredness of small moments, the clarity found in stillness, and the quiet miracles that unfold when one chooses faith over fear. Her intuition, once dismissed, has now become a compass that guides her decisions, relationships, and the life she is building with intention.

This book marks the beginning of Katherine's work as a storyteller, spiritual encourager, and voice for those navigating their own seasons of breaking and rebuilding. She writes with honesty, warmth, and a deep understanding of what it means to fall apart only to rise again stronger, wiser, and more aligned with God's plan.

Katherine hopes her journey will inspire others to trust their intuition, embrace transformation, and believe that they are being guided toward something more meaningful than they could ever have imagined. Her story serves as a reminder that faith can transform pain into purpose, uncertainty into clarity, and adversity into an awakening.